Editors' Letter

This zine marks the end of our chapter as the founding cohort of New Architecture Writers (N.A.W) and the beginning of our transition into Afterparti – a fresh-thinking collective with an event-and-zine series of the same name.

Across these pages, we have attempted to share some of the lessons learnt over the past fifteen-months as N.A.W. In essence, we are unpacking big ideas on contemporary urban space through the lenses of identity and race.

Issue #00, our prototype zine, is an experiment in style, voice and collaboration. It explores the main themes that emerged during our inaugural event, The Time For Failure is Now, including diversity, design colonialism, accountability and education.

Each contributor has developed their articles as a 'response' to statements made during the live event. These statements appear in big, bold lettering, as though a call-to-action.

All nine members of the founding N.A.W cohort have contributed articles in #00. We also invited other thinkers to extend these conversations with us. Our guest contributors include Akil Scafe-Smith of Brixton-based design firm, Resolve, Pooja Agrawal of local planning fast-track initiative, Public Practice, and Joseph Henry from the Greater London Authority.

Their pieces star alongside interviews with Royal Institute of British Architects President Ben Derbyshire and Neba Sere of support network, Black Females in Architecture. We hope that the combination of these unique voices will inspire more debate and extend the afterlife of our original live event.

We have brought Afterparti into the world at a time of gross failure. Scandals such as Brexit, Grenfell, Windrush and the rise of the far right have divided the country and created a climate of tension and paranoia. It is especially meaningful, then, that even as the population prepares for the worst we have received such encouragement and support from so many people.

Thank you wholeheartedly for joining this troupe of nine young writers and thinkers as we test our ideas in the public arena. In finding our feet we have stumbled and stressed, but we have learned to fail better and better!

This is just the beginning.

Afterparti

The Afterparti Collective

Shukri Sultan [5]

is Afterparti's archivist and graphics accomplice. She is doing a Master's degree in Architectural History at the Bartlett and always has a few Yorkshire Gold tea bags on her.

Aoi Phillips [4]

is the graphics tsar and zine coordinator of Afterparti. She is studying for her Diploma at the Architectural Association and, since making this issue, is obsessed with yellow.

Tara Okeke [8]

is Afterparti's interview correspondent. She is a member of Black Female Architects and is also missing a rib.

Marwa El Mubark [6]

is the event reporter for Afterparti. She is the first fully qualified architect of our collective and has an unhealthy obsession with cats.

Thomas Aquilina [3]

is the co-editor and ideas visionary for Afterparti. He is a designer for Adjaye Associates, an itinerant academic and an incessant list-maker.

Samson Famusan[9]

is Afterparti's events coordinator and influencer. He is an architectural designer in an interdisciplinary collective in London and West Africa, and is also afraid of heights.

Josh Fenton[7]

is the numbers man and graphics assistant for Afterparti. He spent two years of his childhood riding skateboards on his belly, and is now studying for his Part 2 at the London School of Architecture.

Siufan Adey[1]

is the co-editor and head commissioner for Afterparti. She is a member of the video team at Dezeen after a degree at the Bartlett, and has an Instagram account for erotic and supernatural Japanese prints.

Nile Bridgeman[2]

is Afterparti's events guru and social media champion. He is notoriously clumsy and is working toward his Part 3 at Ian Chalk Architects.

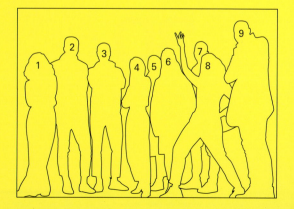

Contents

8 — **The Time for Failure is Now**
A summary of the inaugural event and the Afterparti origin story.

12 — **Equipped with a Moral Compass**
Aoi Phillips examines architecture's potential for violence thorugh design, and the necessity for a moral education.

16 — **Defensive Architecture**
Don't believe everything you read, just take a look for yourself. Armed with his childhood camera **Nile Bridgeman** did just that.

22 — **Quote and Answer Session**
Tara Okeke speaks to **Neba Sere**, one of the four co-founders of the collective Black Females in Architecture (BFA), about some of the most pertinent and provocative thoughts from our live event.

24 — **How Do You Solve a Problem Like the RIBA?**
Siufan Adey brought some of your burning questions to breakfast with RIBA's President, **Ben Derbyshire**.

30 — **Sound Advice: Survival Tips and Tunes for BAME Architects by PAJZH**
Pooja Agrawal co-founded Public Practice and **Joseph Henry** is a Senior Project Officer at the Greater London Authority. The duo are making huge waves in the industry and have teamed-up to offer you some advice on how to survive at the top.

32 Report from the Machinist's Metropolis:

Inspired by Marxist philosopher, Marshall Berman, and architect, Adam Caruso, **Josh Fenton** reveals his dark poetic ruminations on an entity we all know, ignore, and have a hand in sustaining: the Machine.

37 Permanent Infrastructures, Precarious Spaces

Akil Scafe-Smith is the co-founder of Resolve collective, who built a pop-up space inside an abandoned passageway in the Brixton Market from banana boxes. The project led him to discover a dark relationship between fruit and Caribbean identity.

40 East Meets West

The Western University is the most insidious concept you may never have even heard of. **Marwa El Mubark** explains the term, crowned by Ramon Grosfoguel, and how we might free ourselves from it.

44 School(room)'s Out

Having worked as a supply teacher in one of London's poorest schools, **Shukri Sultan** witnessed first hand the effect that design can have on children. Here, she recounts her experience and offers an alternative.

48 Objet Blah

Tara Okeke critiques architecture-as-art in the form of a comic.

50 Escapades in Consciousness

Samson Séyí Famusan reflects on human beings, architecture, and material culture.

54 Figures of Thought

Thomas Aquilina writes a letter to the Royal College of Art's Adrian Lahoud following their conversation on mental health and architecture.

We are enormously grateful to everyone who made our programme possible:

Advisory Board

Shumi Bose, curator and writer
Adrian Lahoud, The Royal College of Art
Lesley Lokko, University of Johannesburg
Priya Khanchandani, Editor of Icon Magazine
Farshid Moussavi, Farshid Moussavi Architecture
David Ogunmuyiwa, ArchitectureDoingPlace

Contributors

Jon Astbury, Barbican Centre
Danah Abdulla, academic
Amanda Baillieu, Archiboo
Peter Barber, Peter Barber Architects
Jonas Berthod, graphic designer
Hunter Charlton, Monocle
Amica Dall, Assemble
Alpa Depani, ROMP zine
Tom Dyckhoff, broadcaster and author
Caz Facey, ING Media
Paul Gorman, writer
Owen Hatherley, writer
Will Hunter, founder of the LSA
Elizabeth Hopkirk, Building Design
Indy Johar, Architecture 00
Douglas Murphy, author and architect
Sophie Lovell, &Beyond
Maki and Associates, architects
Joe Morris, Morris+Company
Manon Mollard, Editor of the Architectural Review
Douglas Murphy, architect and critic
Christine Murray, The Developer
Arman Nouri, Eyesore Magazine
Hugh Pearman, RIBAJ
Francesca Perry, Blueprint magazine
Isabelle Priest, RIBAJ
Jack Self, REAL Foundation
Fiona Shipwright, &Beyond
Cath Slessor, editor and writer
Chloe Spiby Loh, the Architecture Foundation
Tom Ravenscroft, Dezeen
Eleanor Young, RIBAJ
Richard Waite, the Architects' Journal
Danna Walker, Built By Us
Rob Wilson, The Architects' Journal
Anna Winston, writer and consultant
Dave Walker, Kensington & Chelsea Local Studies Collection
Ellis Woodman, Director of the Architecture Foundation

We are a collective born out of... NAW

New Architecture Writers is a free programme for emerging design critics, developing the journalistic skill, editorial connections and voice of its participants. N.A.W. focuses on black and minority ethnic emerging writers who are under-represented across design journalism and curation.

The N.A.W. programme comprises workshops, talks, tours, written briefs and one-to-one mentoring from experienced design critics and editors who give their time voluntarily.

N.A.W. is supported by the Architecture Foundation and the Architectural Review with the Royal College of Art and RIBA Journal.

The programme is made possible thanks to the support of key firms who are committed to fighting discrimination and promoting equality and diversity in the built environment industry.

We Made That
Derwent London
Jestico + Whiles
Baylight Foundation

If you are interested in supporting N.A.W. and the Afterparti collective please email **admin@newarchitecturewriters.org**

N.A.W. is led by Phineas Harper and Tom Wilkinson.

The Time for Failure is Now

'The Time for Failure is Now' was the inaugural event for New Architecture Writers last June. The event acted as a catalyst for a conversation around the topic of failure in architecture, or at least what is considered a failure in our current day profession: failures in education systems, failures in diversifying the profession, and ultimately failures in guarding and maintaining our role as designers and caretakers of our built environment. This magazine is a synthesis of the themes that emerged during the course of the event and a continuation of the conversations it entailed.

Panel Discussion
The panel discussion, chaired by Adrian Lahoud, featured a variety of participants each with their own unique background and perspective. Danah Abdulla, Danna Walker and Indy Johar were joined by David Ogunmuyiwa, Director of ArchitectureDoingPlace and Farshid Moussavi, founder of Farshid Moussavi Architects. David Ogunmuyiwa spoke of Architecture as a 'prosthetic extension' of society that has currently fallen into the grasp of capitalism, while Moussavi advocated for design that is all inclusive because "the world that we design for is diverse". The panel concluded that, despite the many apparent failures of architecture today, there are still opportunities for change – and they start with conversations like this.

From left:
Adrian Lahoud is the Dean of the School of Architecture at the Royal College of Art.

Indy Johar is an architect, commentator, and professor at the University of Sheffield. He also the founder of Dark Matter Laboratories, and co-founded the collaborative studio, Project 00.

David Ogunmuyiwa is the director of ArchitectureDoingPlace and a design associate for the Mayor of London.

Danna Walker is an entrepreneur and founder of the social enterprise, Built by Us. She is a trustee of the Stephen Lawrence Charitable Trust and a board member of the Architects Registration Board.

Dr. Danah Abdulla is a designer and researcher, who lectures at the London College of Communication.

Farshid Moussavi is a celebrated architect and founder of Farshid Moussavi Architects.

"The purpo[se]
architectur[e]
is to disrup[t]
It's not to p[rovide]
fodder for [a]
It has to di[srupt]
practice of

se of
l education
 practice.
rovide
 machine.
rupt the
he future."

Indy Johar

Equipped with a Moral Compass
Examining Architectural Education's Shortfalls
Aoi Phillips

When we think of violence, we associate it with destruction and loss but as architects we are constantly committing the violence of creation. Inevitably we tear down what preceded us or concrete over greenery in our pursuit of the better. The ethical balance of a project's net good is hard to grasp — harder still to measure. The standard metric for net good in the vast majority of projects is economic growth but the violent repercussions of gentrification show the many shortfalls of simply using money to determine the betterment of a place or building.

In our interview, Indy Johar said that as architects and designers "we cannot move forward until we become advocates of other people's realities rather than just advocates of our imaginariums." We need to become adept at inhabiting these other realities. In architectural education we are often trained to achieve some combination of efficiency and beauty — to solve spatial challenges. An element sorely missed is the social and ethical impact of architecture.

Most students and young people are aware of, and are learning about, different structures of power and community-driven design. The pull of our moral compasses is particularly strong while still studying. What kind of architect should we be? A developer? A start-up starter? A community collective? A fancy extension builder? All are valid. The peer pressure to be ethical and 'listening to the people' is powerful in architecture school. Yet very rarely are we ever taught how to begin to do it. How do we engage with the context we seek to build over or warp? Ignoring this question of practice risks the emergence of another generation of architects who are either unequipped to create truly good buildings, or who maintain the illusion of engagement for the audiences of our echo chambers — the architectural crit.

The Pritzker Prize medal features a compass designed by Louis Sullivan on one side. The inscription reads: "FIRMNESS COMMODITY DELIGHT" and directly references the triad of values which the ancient Roman architect and engineer, Vitruvius, believed were at the core of good building. Many generations of architects have already questioned this emphasis on aesthetics. The very fact that our most prestigious award is inscribed with these words suggests we are long overdue scrutinising the values we strive to achieve in society.

We are an increasingly visual culture in a screen age, but technology has also given us a growing forum for the voices of the underrepresented. We cannot continue to make assumptions about what people want and need in regards to our creations. The discernable movement towards establishing equitable collectives over corporations and social justice over business-as-usual, is often dismissed as the naive over-enthusiasm of the young, but it is with this youthful drive towards betterment that we must shape our built environment. Our compasses need to direct us towards the wider values of the people we build for. It is no longer enough to uphold only the most beautiful buildings when even through beauty we have such capacity for violence.

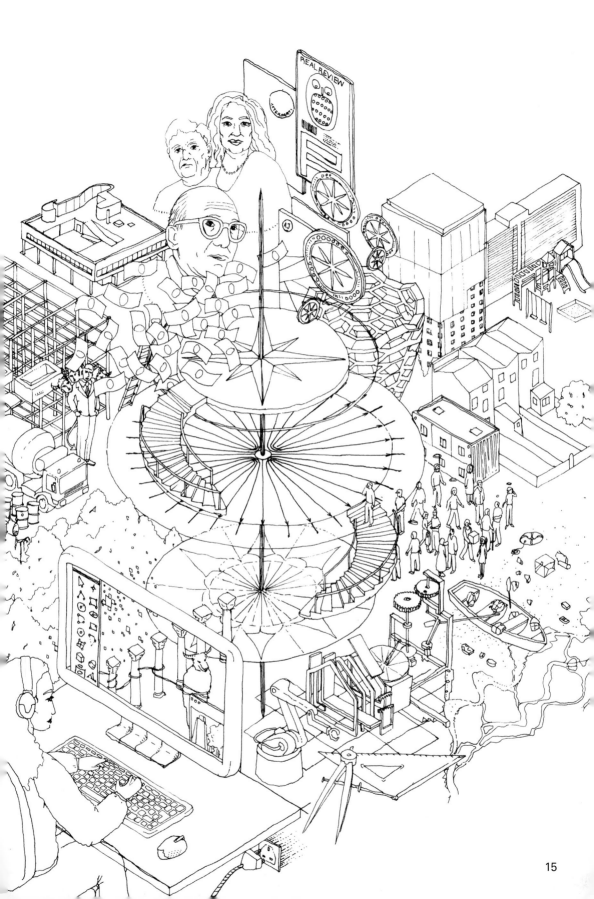

"We have to challenge how spatial and environmental injustice and violence is occurring, everyday."

Indy Johar

Defensive Architecture:
The Architectural Policing of Social Boundaries
Nile Bridgeman

Skate-free seating: Fun-sapping Metal protrusions on surfaces skateboarders are drawn to prioritise economic activity over active engagement with the city.

As the amount of privately owned outdoor space grows, so too does the confusion about what actually constitutes 'public space'. On the surface, these quasi-public spaces appear accessible to all. But, with alarming frequency, they use architecture to define who they want around and more specifically, who they do not want.

The desires of the space's owners and operators are reflected through the deployment of defensive architecture. Implementing a strict 'out of sight, out of mind' policy, they demonstrate a frightening level of indifference towards often disadvantaged sectors of society. This occurs in every city and the solution cannot simply be to push people elsewhere; it does nothing more than displace their distress.

With this hostility comes other problems. Defensive architecture's inability to choose who it impedes and excludes affects us all. Bus stop perches designed to be impossible to sleep on are equally impossible to sit on for anyone pregnant, elderly or frail. Benches throughout Camden boldly claim to have designed out crime and anti-social behaviour and have discomfort designed in instead. Fun-sapping skate-stoppers strip city centres of an opportunity for creative engagement and encounter.

This aggressive approach to the treatment of the public and public space needs to be reversed before cities exclusively consist of sterile, static public places where any activity outside of work or consumption is unwelcome.

This page and overleaf bottom right:
Camden Benches, EC1: Two designs by poster boys of hostile design, Factory Furniture. All claim to prevent crime, litter, nuisance, skateboarding, graffiti and rough-sleeping, as well as sitting for any length, by being deliberately uncomfortable.

Above, from left:
Triple Threat, St Paul's:
A stretch of seating designed to prevent rough-sleeping, planter designed to prevent skateboarding, and handrail so heavily knobbled it fails in its primary purpose, all within feet of each other

Spiked Sill, Fleet Street:
Rough-sleepers are aggressively targeted by this office window. The message being sent to all those looking for shelter is loud and clear

Clockwise:
Spiked Seating, Holborn:
Dwelling is strictly forbidden between a run of shops and offices. Respite can only be found in front of a fire escape

Segregated Seating, Bishopsgate:
The purpose of this seating arrangement is to prevent large groups from forming and spending extended periods of time here, turning this 'public' space into a thoroughfare. Another key feature is its inability to be slept on

Segregated Seating, Shoreditch:
Different seating but the same story. Anti-social at best, and outwardly hostile at worst. They are the embodiment of society's feeling of absolute ambivalence to the suffering of rough-sleepers

Quotation and Answer Session

'Q&A' becomes 'quotation & answer', as **Tara Okeke** turns some of the most urgent and provocative thoughts from our live event into a continuing conversation with an emerging voice in the industry. For Issue #00, we spoke to **NEBA SERE** – one of the four co-founders of the grassroots collective Black Females in Architecture (BFA).

INDY JOHAR: "We can't create accountability until we build a sense of injustice on the ground."

NEBA SERE: BFA was set up last June after a chance meeting between myself and the other three co-founders [Alisha Morenike Fisher, Akua Danso and Selasi Setufe]. First and foremost, we saw it as a means to stay in touch with each other as we all recognised that coming across black women at industry events is a rare occurrence. Eventually, we began to add more black women we personally knew within the built environment field to a WhatsApp group where our conversations often centre on sharing relevant events, employment and creative opportunities, and completed milestones – as well as work or education-related frustrations and advice. We underestimated the need for the group's existence and to our surprise, over a period of four months, the WhatsApp group expanded exponentially and we now have over 170 members.

IJ: "We've gone from seeing humans as an individual object—depicted as the Vitruvian Man and the Modular Man—to this notion that we are interdependent... Human beings are contextual."

NS: I grew up in Germany and undertook my undergrad at RWTH Aachen University. The first year course had around 200 students and I was the only person with black heritage. This issue – the racial disparity – is something I notice now but didn't necessarily think about back then. When I moved to London I became more aware and sought to learn about UK racial histories and larger contextual issues. On one hand I thought it was incredible to see black news presenters on the TV, something which is almost unthinkable in Germany at the moment, but on the other hand, I noticed that the picture was very different within academia, specifically in built environment education. Co-founding BFA is one step towards addressing this.

Co-founder of BFA, Neba Sere

DANAH ABDULLA: "It's a power dynamic. Who has the power?"

NS: Those with power should offer platforms and opportunities to people or groups with less power for them to be able to access vital (but, more often than not, unattainable) resources and systems. That can be as simple as providing access to a space for a meeting or assisting with the development of organisational strategies in regards to business or finance. Helping a less established group with "the basics" will enable those groups to have the right tools in place to really reach a wider audience and thus have a wider impact.

DANNA WALKER: "I think it's inevitable that I am a role model for some black women. You just need to look at the figures. Thousands of people qualify in architecture each year. Around ten of those people are black, and of that number only a small proportion are women. It is such a tiny pool — we're like diamonds or something!"

NS: Within our research, we have noticed that the US is much more advanced than the UK when it comes to gathering statistics about under-represented groups… We don't even know who the first UK registered black female architect was or the first to teach at a university. [BFA] have made it one of our goals this year to pull together a research team to gather those statistics and histories, and maybe in the future we can look at something similar to Tiffany Brown's '400 Forward'.

IJ: "Some people will say, 'But everything's getting better.' No dude! The fact is that there is a fundamental discrepancy in the social contract… The discrepancy is between the discourse and the underlying reality — and [it's] massively visible."

NS: We have noticed this within our own network's discussions and dynamics. One can also easily get lost in talking about all the things that should be better for POC or all the injustices that have happened but that isn't necessarily empowering or doesn't look forward. As a way to tackle this, we are very keen on doing other things apart from socials and meetups where we only talk within our community. I believe the strength of our network is showing or proving the fact that we are capable designers, architects, engineers, academics etc. to make our actions speak louder than our words.

We are now actively looking into running small scale projects and have created a smaller team made up of a few co-founders and a few BFA members who will manage and deliver projects together. In the long run, we would like those BFA members to lead projects themselves and initiate new projects and collaborations.

DW: "When you're a person from a diverse background, there is more pressure to do well, to make your family proud, to not be the one that messes up. But some of the greatest lessons you learn are through failure."

NS: My upbringing was focused on doing well at school, having good grades and then continuing to study medicine, law or engineering at university. I went down the creative route which did raise a few eyebrows within my family and culminated in recurring questions about whether I'd be able to sustain a living as an architect, a question which, honestly, I am still not able to answer today. Throughout my educational and professional life, I often seem to be the lone black woman and it sometimes feels as if my actions, successes or failures are a poster for what we as black women are only capable of. In the light of this, I've developed a high expectations of myself to deliver.

Within architecture, I define success as 'being the first at doing something' and to have a bigger aim than doing things merely for fun, recognition or aesthetics, to make sure the profession improves. The conception of BFA propelled us to being observed by 170 other women as role-models, mentors and collaborators, and so we believe in maintaining a good public reputation. But because this is a new organisation where we are still learning to manage ourselves, failure is inevitable. Personally, I am still getting used to accepting the fact that things will not go the right way the first time but that everything is a work in progress and that failure is part of the necessary journey to making things better.

ADRIAN LAHOUD: "There's always a struggle over control of the future's infrastructure, without which the visions for the future would be meaningless. Struggle really reverberates in the background of the idea of failure. So much of what we take for granted was built on the backs of long struggles that we've forgotten about."

NS: Currently, I'm training to be an architect for which I have to practice under the Architects Registration Board's Architects Code, which is made up of 12 standards of professional conduct and practice. It mentions attitudes and attributes that are expected from architects such as being honest, working with integrity, professionalism and having respect for others to name a few. But interestingly there is very little mention of a social responsibility, which I believe is key to the success of the practice of an architect in today's progressing world.

I see the emergence of BFA as one step further into diversifying the architect's profession.

"I would like RIBA to stop glorifying good buildings and instead talk about social and spatial injustice across the UK"

Indy Johar

How Do You Solve a Problem Like the RIBA?
Bringing your burning questions to RIBA president, Ben Derbyshire
Siufan Adey

The man who sits across the table from me in a two-tone blue-and-red knitted tie and yellow tweed jacket is the face of the RIBA and the UK's architectural profession. "I am the Chair of the board and the Chair of the council," declares Ben Derbyshire, clicking the heels of his brogues together.

My puddle-soaked Doc Martens, however, remain firmly affixed to the floor – as if this gesture of defiance might help me resist being cajoled by his magnetic exuberance and offerings of pain au chocolat.

It's a miserable morning in January but the reasons I find myself in Derbyshire's vibrant interdisciplinary Shoreditch practice can be traced back to the previous summer's event The Time For Failure is Now. Throughout the day, the RIBA was mentioned several times by both audience members and speakers alike, so I took it upon myself to present some of these questions to the man at the top.

Derbyshire took up the position of President of the RIBA after the 2016 election in which a mere 15.2% of members participated. Of this number, 53.8% voted for him. Assuming the organisation had around the same 43,000-strong membership it has today, then Derbyshire actually only represents about 3,500 architects.

"If you criticise the profession – and the institute that represents it – for not being relevant to your needs then you've only got yourselves to blame," argues Derbyshire, pounding the table. While this would have been an outrageous accusation just a couple of years ago, the recent organisation-wide shake-up has started to lend this some truth.

Derbyshire's presidency is founded upon his campaign called #ChangeIsNecessary, and has attempted to address architectural education, diversity in the profession, the value of architects within society, and the structure of the institute. But has this white, middle class, Cambridge-educated son-of-an-architect actually managed to effect any change?

"At the time I was elected the average age of RIBA members was 57 years old but now it's decreasing," he says proudly. This is due in part, he claims, to the enfranchisement of its young members. In the next presidential election, student members will be allowed to vote, which Derbyshire predicts will radically transform the institute, since the needs of architecture students are routinely neglected to the detriment of their mental and physical health, financial stability, and quality of life.

"I've never ever ever done an all-nighter in my life!" Derbyshire exclaims before launching into a lengthy diatribe in which no cornerstone of architecture school is left unturned: the traditional 'crit' is discriminatory, irrelevant, and should make way for more motivational round-the-table discussions; educators and practitioners, who are currently at loggerheads, need to gain mutual understanding of one another's aims; lecture content is desperately stale and should embrace myriad interdisciplinary topics. The list goes on.

"A university degree should inculcate the core competences and necessary understandings for a long term career," he insists. "Which, by the way, isn't about creating oven-ready CAD-fodder. We want creatives and critical thinkers who understand business realities."

If architectural education is so fucked up, then why hasn't anything changed? "The government have decreed that our regulator, the Architects Registration Board, shall not make any changes to architectural education," he retorts bitterly. "They want all of the legislature that applies to ARB to hop over to RIBA."

As for the serious lack of diversity in the profession and in schools? "Just one percent of British students finishing their architectural training are black compared to the eight percent who enter first year," he begins, "I think that the missing seven percent worked out the math, quite frankly."

He goes on to explain that a mid-career salary for an architect is £45,000 per year, while a self-employed practitioner of the same standing will earn an average of £23,000 per year. Set this against hundreds of thousands of pounds' worth of student debt – with little to no familial support – and that's a very poor equation.

But rather than releasing more funding to low-income families, of which a disproportionate number are BAME, Derbyshire has attempted to solve the diversity problem by way of a long-term quixotic strategy of raising the status of all architects in society. "The root of the problem is that society regards architects as an eccentric absurdity and is not availing itself of our skills," he continues. Perhaps #AllArchitectsMatter would've been a more appropriate campaign title.

Two main concepts for reinstating the architect were elaborated on in our conversation: post-occupancy valuation, and a new Code of Conduct.

Firstly, post-occupancy valuation may become mandatory as a result of Derbyshire's presidency, which he claims will "hold architects to account". A set of criteria would be taken down at the very beginning of the design process for the outcomes that the building is intended to deliver. These objectives would be monitored through all of the work stages. One year, two years and five years after completion, the building would undergo a rigorous evaluation of whether or not it has succeeded in achieving these outcomes.

The criteria would be integrated into the conditions of Stirling Prize, which is a powerful window into the profession and its values. "No building will be considered for an award unless the architect and the client have signed up to a post-occupancy evaluation," Derbyshire declares, hammering his point into the table with his fist again.

Secondly, Derbyshire has commissioned a review for the architects' code of conduct and code of practice. "Post-Grenfell, can you seriously argue that as a profession we should not be putting the public interest at the heart of everything we do? The calamity of Grenfell was not just the construction process and the

> "There's a massive problem in terms of race and class. What is RIBA doing to address this? What can be done?"
>
> Sahra Hersi, Audience member

design process failing to put the interest of the people living in that building above all else but the whole thing was a perfect storm of failure." A code of conduct which makes public interest mandatory would give chartered architects the backing to refuse to engage with work that does not incorporate these values, he claims.

"We've completely rewritten the constitution which dates from 1834," he continues. "By the time my successor takes over, there'll be a much simpler and freer constitution. It will be much better resourced, much better run and much lighter of foot".

The process only began when Derbyshire took office. "It was good timing, I suppose," he shrugs. "One of our subsidiaries, RIBA Enterprises, came to us asking for investment and we ran a competition for an equity partner who was able to invest in both the subsidiary and its parent – the RIBA itself." With this money, the RIBA was able to rid itself of debt and better position itself to weather a long overdue shake-up.

But even with the RIBA's newfound revenue – which by the way is in the tens of millions – Derbyshire refuses to reduce membership costs. "Advancing architecture is our purpose. We're not about looking after our members like a trade union," he insists. "We're not going to reduce the price of the subscription. We need to be a high-value organisation capable of reasonably charging £400 per annum and I make no apology for that."

In response to the questions raised at last summer's event, Derbyshire's message is clear: participate and have a hand in creating a stable, effective institute, or let one of architecture's biggest resources crumble into decrepitude. The man who sits across the table from me appears to have blown away some cobwebs in the mechanics of the organisation. Do these changes amount to the dawning of a new age for the RIBA or are they the equivalent of a bright knitted tie – eye-catching, but impractical bling? •

Failure from the Archives
[Erased] Barandon Street, (South side),
10th July 1969

North Kensington's treatment of its poor inhabitants in synonymous with failures such as Rachmanism, the 1958 race riots, social cleansing and mostly recently the tragedy of Grenfell. It's failures are rooted in social injustice and misaligned priorities. Perhaps the most embarrassing failure in recent years is that since 1990, the Royal Borough of Kensington and Chelsea has only built 10 social homes.

Images property of The Kensington and Chelsea Local Studies
Text: Shukri Sultan

Sound

Survival Tips and Tunes for BAME Architects
by PAJZH (F.K.A. Pooja Agrawal and Joseph Henry)

Be grateful when you are invited to participate in public talks – even if it is only a desperate attempt by the organisers to fill the diversity gap.

**Mr Eazi
Pour me Water**

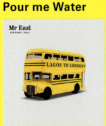

Look glam whilst networking. The photographer will inevitably snap photos of you to capture "diversity".

**SZA
Drew Barrymore**

Avoid wearing cultural garb on site, you'll never be taken seriously otherwise.

**Jimothy
Fashion**

Do laugh when colleagues make fun of your name. You wouldn't want them to think you don't have a sense of humour.

**Erykah Badu
On & On**

Pretend you're listening to Radio 4's Desert Island Discs in the office instead of Tierra Whack on repeat.

**Tierra Whack
Flea Market**

When clients ask where you are from, don't say "Tooting" because it will always be followed by the question: "But where are you really from?"

**Stormzy
Know Me From**

Be patient with contractors, site managers and anyone who fails to comprehend that you are actually the person in charge.

**Serine Karthage
Ruler**

If you can't be arsed to listen to colleagues bang on about their projects, just convince them they have you confused with the only other BAME colleague in your organisation.

**Skepta
That's Not Me ft. JME**

Don't start social media wars on the subject of discrimination in architecture – white extremist bots will be the politest responses you'll receive.

**The Internet
Look What You Started**

You're not cool even if everyone says you're cool. It's just a white architect's adjective for 'brown architect'.

**Digable Planets
Rebirth of Slick
(Cool like dat)**

Advice:

Get used to being called "scary" if you are in a position of power.

**Nadia Rose
On Top**

For your entertainment: when a colleague asks whether you've heard of a specific grime artist, foreign actor, or non-white architect, tell them you don't know who they are – just to fuck with them. Sigh. It's the small wins.

**Jamila Woods
Lonely ft. Lorine Chia**

Feel lucky to be included in a write-up about any event, initiative or building that you have created.

**Dawn Richard
We, Diamonds**

Keep calm when audience members repeatedly quote your idea but miscredit it to the white male panel member.

**IAMDBB
Shade**

Don't be surprised if you're asked to move from the seat reserved for the guest speakers. God forbid you might actually be the guest speaker.

**Kaytranada
Leave Me Alone ft. Shay Lia**

Never flag the compère who follows your introduction with "isn't it great we have such a diverse panel?"

**Beyoncé
Formation**

Don't roll your eyes when people comment on how much better things are now than they used to be.

**Loyle Carner
Ain't Nothing Changed**

Your success is only a result of tokenism. It's not like you actually earned it after having to work twice as hard as your white counterparts.

**Blood Orange
You're Not Good Enough**

Never write articles about diversity in the profession. Diversity will become your pigeonholed area of expertise.

**Neneh Cherry
Natural Skin Deep**

You are the definition of the "new architectural professional". Be proud.

**Solange
Don't Touch My Hair**

"We have to become political in the sense of guardianship. And that will build the space for all of us as architects to act more responsibly."

Indy Johar

Report from the Machinist's Metropolis:
A Summary of How it is Now
Josh Fenton

The Machine, referenced here, is an entity that appears to be living, driven by conscious rationale, but it is only kept animated by capital. Its output varies, but consistently these are cover-all, catch-all solutions, seemingly designed to fail. As it lumbers forward, under the operating hand of builders and planners, following the design of speculators, the effects are beginning to seep into our everyday experience.

Architects of the early twentieth century maintained an altruistic hope of building a new, accessible utopia[1]. Back then, they were free from obligation and servility to The Machine – or perhaps they chose not to pay heed to its stirrings. In practice however, The Machine always had its way and The Altruistic Architects' intentions were not always realised. This is most apparent in the case of social housing, where some estates came to be defined by social unrest and squalor.

One example of a post-war aspirational housing scheme that became synonymous with slums and sink estates is the Le Corbusier-inspired Broadwater Farm Estate in Tottenham, North London. Just five years after its completion in 1973, the complex developed a catalogue of maintenance issues: rubbish-chutes hosted cockroaches and vermin, and poor weather protection led to significant damp in many flats. In 1985, it fell further into decline, providing a harrowing backdrop to scenes of riots. The graphic and symbolic power of its architecture became its downfall. Its visibility placed it centre stage, serving as a scapegoat for underlying political and social issues. There is a strange irony in how Le Corbusier saw his rationalist approach as the solution to the distress brought on by The Machine's desires, observing that, "the country today is harsh, unattractive, tyrannical: the money civilization by which modern society has blackened and deflowered, has extended its grip to the peasant and made his life a barren, sooty thing"[2].

A cloud of apathy seems to have fallen over many of our fellow architects, who no longer question why they are called upon to put things right within a framework that is wholly wrong, or why they should beautify things that are anything but. Instead we march along gangways and monitor the production line long-sufferingly, keeping everything ticking over - the packaged product maintaining the dream that one day we can all perpetually promenade in anaesthetised bliss.

We try to feign ignorance of the fact that these promises are rarely fulfilled. Instead, we grope around in the digested scrap and shrapnel. We become buried by the ever-mounting wastage of speculation. "Look at this new piece of city!" we cheer as we stand proudly atop the rubble of another neglected housing project. "Look at the positive change this development has delivered!" But pay no mind to the deafening roar of the void just over there.

Seeking further expansion of its mechanical production line, The Machine now lurches towards the borough of Newham, in East London. With a White British population of 16%, the term 'ethnic minority' is practically defunct – 103 languages are spoken within the area and 45% of the residents were born outside of

Above: the 1985 riots

[1] Eric J. Cesal, Down Detour Road: An Architect In Search of Practice. Cesal notes that we have gone from unlicensed "master masons" to registered architects wielding little power.

[2] Deborah Gans, 'Big Work: Le Corbusier and Capitalism' in Ed. Peggy Deamer Architecture and Capitalism: 1845 to the Present.

Britain. This international miscellany is set against a backdrop of historic cycles of reinvention and decline. In fact, the arrival of migrants first began after the closure of the Royal Albert Docks in the early 1980s massively cheapened housing costs in the area.

Despite, or perhaps because of, the poverty that exists in the area, the intervening period has seen a specific and distinct set of characteristics developed by locals. Together they have created a place where traditional pubs sit alongside Lithuanian food stores on Plaistow High Street, and a Ghanaian-Anglican church and local mosque address the same street corner. This tapestry of interactions is currently being overlooked in favour of industrial-scale redevelopment. The Mayor of London, Sadiq Khan, has outlined his vision for Newham as the "New Heart for London".

To create this vision, The Machine demands a hefty £22 billion of capital input in return for new development in and around the former Royal Docks site, and the regeneration of Canning Town in the south of the borough. Most recently, a further £1.1billion investment has been secured to fund 'East Bank' within the Olympic Park. The site will provide a home for organisations such as Sadler's Wells, the BBC, London College of Fashion and the Victoria and Albert Museum. As usual, the masterplan comes with an attached perfunctory promise, that it will build upon – rather than erode – the artistic community in Hackney Wick, forming "a new powerhouse of culture, education, innovation and growth".[3]

The problem with The Machine's output, as is often the case, is that it is roughly hewn and too poorly articulated to deal with the real problems at hand. The masterplan is a collaboration between three architecture firms: Allies and Morrison, O'Donnell + Tuomey, and Camps Felip Arquitecturia. On closer inspection, however, it appears to be anything but masterful. Of course, there is ambition at the heart of this project, everything looks suitably shiny and new, and the renders do have the requisite number of couples walking around arm-in-arm, but what isn't addressed is how the arts and education programmes on offer

[3] 'Mayor unveils £1.1bn vision for East Bank', https://www.london.gov.uk/press-releases/mayoral/ mayor-unveils-11bn-vision-for-east-bank,

This page: Broadwater Farm Ziggurat, view looking north; A 1970s brochure for Broadwater Farm.

will be made truly accessible or how the numerous developments tackle the significant social issues at stake in Newham.

Here we have an area where 37% of residents are living in poverty and 4,500 homeless households are currently being sheltered in temporary accommodation. Yet The Machine hastily churns out a solution and 'airdrops' it nearby. Fundamental deficiencies exist, but the correct solutions seem to elude us in a manner not too dissimilar from the processes that contributed to the eruption of violence in Broadwater Farm. Phased regeneration could be a solution, but it is a time-consuming and, therefore, costly procedure. Newham council seems to prefer a clean, precision-engineered product, that delivers attractive metrics and press headlines. Therefore, despite the first phase of the Stratford and Olympic Park regeneration delivering 1,350 'affordable' homes, Newham still has the highest number of residents relocated outside of London. The situation becomes even more confusing when we see the number of homes left abandoned in Canning Town. Despite the clamour of The Machine starting up in Stratford, we must question why the slew of new funding is not being utilised to renovate or reprogram these spaces.

The appetite for a nuanced understanding of physical, social and cultural assets seems to have dissipated. Even if the desire exists, there simply isn't time. We hurriedly try to keep pace, pulling chords and flicking switches, trying to maintain our precarious place. Perhaps in a moment of clarity, we will realise that The Machine needs people to operate it – Machinists if you will – and as such, we have a level of control over quality. Failures should be a signal to question the processes we operate, their sequence, and the output itself. As for how it is now, we are busy – servicing the entity that will bring about our own downfall. •

This page: The Tangmere Shopping Arcade failed to recover its former glory after the riots.

Above: The zeal with which 2012's trophy projects began, has not been maintained.

Failure from the Archives
Demolition Site, Lancaster Road (East Side)

27th July 1969

As part of the post-war slum clearance programme, large areas of North Kensington were demolished to make way for the Westway and new housing estates such as the Lancaster West Estate. However, had these houses remained, they would soon have become some of the most sought-after properties in London. In total 15% of all homes in England were demolished as part of the slum clearance, creating a mass migration of the working class population.

Images property of The Kensington and Chelsea Local Studies
Text: Shukri Sultan

Permanent Infrastructures, Precarious Spaces
On banana boxes, fruit trade and Caribbean identity
Akil Scafe-Smith

"Yuh tink tings woulda change by now. My grandfadda's grandfadda come a Jamaica in the hold of a ship. My mudda did run away to Cuba inna the twenties fi cut cane, and I came here. It must be some kinda curse that condemn our people fi wander the earth like ghost who cyan find nuh rest." - Obeah Woman.

This passage from Winsome Pinnock's 1987 play, 'Leave Taking', alludes to a complex relationship that has defined Caribbean movement for centuries. It encompasses both the generative historical experience of slavery in the Black Atlantic and more contemporary migratory events such as early 20th century intra-Caribbean migration and the exodus of the Windrush generation. Pinnock's words describe a unique relationship between capital and the movement of bodies; between places and their connections; and between the built environment and its discontents. They exemplify a narrative whereby movement is not a vehicle of diaspora, but rather its determinant, and posit its architectures and infrastructures – the holds of ships, colonial enclaves, council estates, railway arches, and banana boxes – as parameters of a Sisyphean labour rather than an emancipatory struggle. Amidst the ostensible success stories of migration in the West today, and as our cities become both spaces of unparalleled diversity and violent inequity, it is our duty as practitioners, theorists, consumers, and observers to challenge the devaluation of spaces that are significant for diasporic communities and the obscuring of the histories of "ghosts who cyan find nuh rest".

Our design research, which interrogates the varying scales of spatial organisation underpinning human movement, questions the assumed fixity of Caribbean identity, suggesting instead that it has been largely defined by flows of labour, commerce, and cultural capital. As such, mobility and syncretism are key tenets to Caribbean diasporic identity, though this is often concurrent with a socio-spatial asymmetry whereby spaces that are central to the diaspora are starkly less resilient than the social and physical infrastructures that precipitate them.

This imbalance is explored in the present case of Brixton and the historical case of the Banana Republics of the Caribbean and Latin America. This piece concludes by suggesting that designing with a more nuanced understanding of Caribbean diasporic identity may engender new methods of mitigating the processes that threaten these spaces.

Boxes in Brixton

"If you're regretting the fact that your housekeeping allowance won't stretch to a seat on the next plane Trinidad bound," chimes the voice of an antiquated commentator in a 1961 Pathé documentary on Brixton Market, "take a trip to London South West Nine". Decades after Pathe's jaunt down to SW9 Brixton Market continues to be an epicentre of Caribbean culture in London, with crowds of West Indian mothers still queueing to buy fish in Holy Week, and with string vests, Conquering Lions of Judah, yams, and patties still defining its mise-en-scène. Now, however, the market is being threatened with intractable change as a result of gentrification and rapacious land speculation.

Our project 'Passageway' was conceived of as a temporary space in which questions of the social, historic, political, cultural, and environmental value of urban markets in our increasingly valorised cities constituted both the project's core programmatic ambitions and its spatial skein. Within a derelict space in Brixton Market we repurposed hundreds of banana boxes from the market, transforming an essential component of market infrastructure into a new internal structure that provided an armature for conversation, performances, exhibitions, food events, and workshops.

The structure was designed to reflect the tactility of these banana boxes in their original setting. The boxes are in many ways the currency of space in Brixton Market rarely containing bananas, but instead becoming tables, chairs and display plinths by day, and storage cupboards, shelters and bins by night. Their resilience stands in stark contrast to the volatile circumstances of the surrounding businesses and vendors.

Together with the boxes' impressive propensity for appropriation, their greatest appeal is their striking beauty: some of the boxes feature heavily stylised images of idyllic Caribbean landscapes while

Boxes in Brixton (Image Credit: Vishnu Jay)

From Top: Image courtesy of McGill University, Montreal; Plantations in Limon;

others are imageless, blending austere graphic forms and shapes with royal blues, pink corals, leaf greens, and pineapple yellows to invoke the sensorial Caribbean. The designs are accompanied by the names of a select few countries: Colombia, Honduras, Costa Rica, and Ecuador make frequent appearances, with the occasional Guatemala and Nicaragua. Very rarely do the graphics mention countries such as Trinidad, Jamaica and Barbados or the other islands that populate the collective global imagination of the archetypal West Indies. What's more, the producers of these objets d'art went primarily by four names: Chiquita, Dole, Fyffes, and Del Monte.

In the months that followed the completion of 'Passageway', a question still lingered in our minds: why was the archetypal space of Caribbean identity in London constructed from Latin American banana boxes?

Plantations in Limon

In the early 20th century, the global banana trade was controlled by the United Fruit Company (UFCO), a large American corporation, which had such a stranglehold on the Caribbean and Latin America that many argue it was a form of American crypto-colonialism in the region. UFCO set parameters that shaped entirely novel geographies of labour and capital in the Caribbean and Latin America. Though the company controlled agricultural production in the region through the coercion of political leaders and military factions, its primary means of control was the implementation of vast amounts of infrastructure and ownership over the territories that this dissected. This infrastructural yoke not only transformed the Caribbean coastal regions of Latin America into tributary states of a voracious American food industry but also guided and facilitated the movement of an entire generation of black British West Indians who had left home to labour in what became known as the Banana Republics: Colombia, Honduras, Costa Rica, Ecuador, Panama, Nicaragua, and Guatemala.

Contrasting poetically with the permanence and fixity of colonial infrastructure in the Banana Republics was the ephemerality and mobility of black British West Indians, engendered by their relative youth and the stagnant post-emancipation economies of their homelands. For UFCO, these labourers formed a dependable yet expendable workforce, seen as guaranteed supply of young resilient workhands with no apparent desire to naturalise and whose sovereign rights were largely abandoned by the British Crown. Life in this way was often insufferable and the group was subjected to numerous racist campaigns, economic repression and even deportation. Their living conditions were often deplorable: the spaces in which they resided were designed for infrastructural resilience and human precarity. "A banana plantation is a poor place to live unless you're a banana," wrote one contemporary commentator. Additionally, their presence in these spaces was – and arguably still is – selectively ignored. As Echeverri-Gent points out: "The Central America of books, and indeed of our imaginations, does not have very many black actors"

However, the group's movement formed the basis for a syncretic Caribbean identity that eschewed the physical confines of an island's shore and aligned instead with the interminable ocean and its moving currents. During this period, familial and social networks were spread across the Caribbean and the Latin American coast. Dialects and aesthetics converged, and places became intrinsically connected through song, poetry, and spiritualism. Consequently, Latin American cities such as Colon, Limon, Puerto Cortés, and Bluefield are still characterised by their remarkably Afro-Caribbean identity. Similarly, generations of children in the former British West Indies will have grown up with a sense of the Hispanic reaches of the Caribbean as a recurrent cultural motif through folksongs and poems such as 'Colon Man' and the story of Solomon's Grandpa.

As both a means and a destination, the architectures of social and physical mobility in the region, such as the railway infrastructures, shipping docks, and the banana plantations themselves, became sites by which black West Indian migration transposed the geographic bounds of the Caribbean with oceanographic ones. The wider Caribbean became a web of superimposed, syncretic cultures that both shaped and were shaped by black West Indian identity. Importantly, this period also concretized a culture of mobility that would manifest once more in future, larger migrations such as the Windrush generation to Britain and generational movement to the United States and Canada.

PORTS AND PIERS OF THE GREAT WHITE FLEET
New York...New Orleans...California Service...West Indies...Central and South America

Image courtesy of Gordon Shunway

Infrastructural Resilience, Spatial Precarity

Folded into the parametrics of diasporic space in the early 20th century Caribbean were colonial governance structures that necessitated asymmetries of wealth and ownership, as well as precarity and permeance. Demonstrably, these imbalances are not dissimilar to the asymmetries that threaten Brixton Market's centrality to the Caribbean diaspora of London. Both can be read, albeit on different scales, through the construction of space.

Today, the Banana Republics are still the world's leading banana exporters. Though UFCO no longer exists, its successor, Chiquita, has filled the space it left, together with the three other banana boxes brands found in Brixton, known in the industry as 'The Wild Bunch'. These companies now control 65% of the global banana trade and their boxes surreptitiously populate precarious urban spaces of pronounced cultural significance like Brixton Market. Their presence discloses an asymmetry whereby diasporic identity inauspiciously rests – quite literally – on unwavering commercial infrastructures in urban spaces.

This rings as true for the containers that construct an urban market as it does for the railways and shipping routes that constructed an entire region. Yet, the boxes also offer a lens through which we may understand fluidity – rather than fixity – as a motif of Caribbean diasporic identity. This in turn provides a conceptual and practical foundation for addressing the precarity of diasporic spaces through design in cities today.

In understanding this far more complex relationship between a diaspora and the spaces of significance to them, we may begin to ask at least two more nuanced questions in our collective practices. Firstly, how might we as designers benefit from looking at city-wide, national and international networks of resilient cultural spaces that inform and facilitate one another, rather than individual bastions of culture? Secondly, can we as sufferers re-appropriate notions of temporariness, mobility, and malleability to imagine spaces that cannot be threatened by challenges to their fixed spatial determination and design spaces that do not rest?

"The educational system as a whole needs to change. Change comes from you. At the same time, it also come from us as educators."

Danah Abdulla

Between East and West

How to decolonise design in the East
Marwa El Mubark

In the 1976 novel, 'Roll of Thunder Hear My Cry' by Mildred D. Taylor, the life of an African-American girl, Cassie Logan, is depicted, with all the struggles she endured in growing up in lower-class America during the Great Depression. The book recently made it to America's top 100 classics for children. However, this belated recognition has sparked a deeper reflection on bias in educational systems – a bias which was alluded to by Danah Abdulla at the inaugural New Architecture Writers event in June 2018.

"The educational system as a whole needs to change. In Western universities colonial thinking still exists, and these structures are actually being replicated in the global South. Change comes from you. At the same time, it also come from us as educators. We need to be introducing new ideas to students in the classroom and questioning the social theories that are already on the curriculum."

Growing up, I had always wondered why my education was limited to certain canons of work. I lived in a Western country, so I had assumed I would be taught about Western poets and Western writers from that country. There was a presumption that if an audience is predominantly European then this is what the curriculum should broadly cater to. But what does this mean for minorities growing up in the West and, more importantly, why is the Western experience presented as universal, while the experiences of other cultures – such as the African-American culture in 'Roll of Thunder Hear my Cry' – is considered niche reading and somehow out of the grasp of general consumption?

The Puerto Rican sociologist Ramon Grosfoguel refers to this sociological construct as the 'Westernised University' – a global structure or system under which we all live. It describes a formula of 'epistemological racism' that seeks to label works beyond a limited palette as irrelevant. According to Grosfoguel, these ideals originate from a set of five European countries, whose population makes up just under twelve percent of the global population. After 500 years of European colonial expansion, the Westernised University is no longer limited to the West but has spread to the East. Grosfoguel argues the same canons can now be found in a school in Rio De Janeiro and in Beijing, due to a shared colonial history promoting eurocentric ideals. The Westernised University thrives on the presumption that this narrow focus will create the lens through which the rest of the world will observe and derive their experiences even if the rest of the world has a very different everyday contextual experience.

The ramifications of this situation can be seen in the contemporary architecture of the Middle East. Western design philosophies and values often find expression through built forms that are ill suited to their context. Middle Eastern architects, who have been educated in the Modernist western vocabulary of concrete and glass, produced buildings that are unable to cope with the climatic demands of the region. The legacies of traditional architects practising in an indigenous manner, such as Egyptian architect Hassan Fathy whose architecture was concerned with the social, economic and cultural conditions of 1940s Egypt, have been surpassed in favour of Western principles, which have limited relevance in that context.

So what are the solutions? Grosfoguel suggests that change has only been achieved successfully in the past by means of strike action and revolution. He cites the 1969 Civil Rights movement in America as an example of a situation where uprising was necessary to gain the attention of established institutions at the time. The movement forced universities such as Berkeley and Columbia to give space in recognition of the role that black people played in American society and recognise Ethnic Studies and African-American Studies as subjects in their own right.

Similarly, in Egypt, Fathy revolted against imported westernism by promoting an indigenous architecture rooted in humanism and local heritage. At the heart of his work is the principle that architecture is for humans, and that humans are not interchangeable. They require architecture that is responsive to their psychological and cultural needs as well as their physical needs. He particularly rejected the elements of Modernism that tried to unify the world into a common pattern of living. For example, the assembly line approach seen in Modernism's delivery of mass housing, with its repetition of units in an array across a site, was particularly disdained. Fathy's rejection of imported architecture went beyond a simple rejection of western cultural heritage, but was a rejection of internationalism itself which he saw as a homogenising concept that stripped individuals of their identity.

The East must revolutionize its approach to architecture. As Danah Abdulla argues, "change comes from you". While the physical act of revolting through civil action can go a long way towards garnering attention, I believe that what is needed in the Middle East and wider Global South is a revolution of the mind. The recognition that the outward expression of our thoughts is a direct by-product of our education and upbringing is the first step. We must unravel the effects that the Western University has had on us as individuals. Cultural context and local vernacular need a revival, and should always outweigh externally-imposed ideals, lest we risk a type of creeping cultural genocide. There is no harm in borrowing ideas externally, but our yardstick should be the cultural sensibilities our context has to offer, much more so than arid historic Modernist rhetoric.

In defending cultural authenticity, Fathy emphasized that there is an essential non-interchangeability of cultures. By that he meant that basic cultural elements developed in response to indigenous needs, environmental and psychological, and that alien elements cannot be implanted or transplanted from other cultures or other environments if they are culturally inappropriate. Culturally inappropriate elements that are so inserted into the fabric of the harmonious built environment will undoubtedly generate contradictions, and will, with time, corrode and degrade the traditional culture.

As a society, the East must ultimately recognise its failures and the impact they have had on its culture and identity. This is the first step towards recovery, and often the most difficult in a society which synonymises imitation of the

West with progression. Fathy was a revolutionary in his own right who rejected the professional norms upheld by imported capitalism's architecture, façades and townscapes. He searched for an architecture that was original and rooted in the culture of the region – one that relied on natural resources of mud, stone and earth, and all the building techniques which accompany it. His manifesto includes the message that, in solving human problems, one must not remove oneself too far from the human individual and that the simplicities inherent in the very nature of building must not be overlaid by the worship of progress.

Dar-Ul-Islam Mosque, New Mexico, Hassan Fathy, opened in 1982.

"I've actually never seen so much momentum around social mobility, diversity and inclusion but it's still not enough."

Danna Walker

School(room)'s Out

On Rethinking + Redesigning Our Educational Spaces
Shukri Sultan

The putrid stench of dead rodents hangs over the classrooms of dilapidated Victorian buildings, which were designed for efficient surveillance and control over children. These are the spaces that we provide as a backdrop to social mobility.

Education is often presented as the main tool for social mobility; it was the holy mantra of Tony Blair and the provision of 'good schools for all' was one of Theresa May's unfulfilled promises. Yet this ailing system within its archaic buildings is ill-equipped to carry out these pledges. How can architects rectify this?

The system has failed, and its failure is disproportionately affecting the most disadvantaged children. This is evident in the widening attainment gap. This persistent marked difference in academic achievement between the rich and the poor can be seen throughout the entire system, from early years to higher education.

Reports have shown that by the age of five, children from a disadvantaged background are five months behind their affluent peers in cognitive development. This then increases to nineteen months by the end of GCSE, which are taken at the ages of 15 and 16 years old. Researchers at Stanford University have recorded that the gap is cumulative and starts at birth. The first sign is a gap in language acquisition evident at just eighteen months old.

To address this manifest inequality, the entire system has to be re-thought; what we teach, how we teach and where we teach. The former two are often debated, but the latter is frequently overlooked. The discourse around the educational crisis has failed to address the failures within the architecture of the educational setting itself.

Children are particularly sensitive to their environment, which has tremendous implications on their development. The ability to move freely around space is crucial in the early years of a child. It is linked to intellectual growth, brain development and even eyesight. Architecture that advocates for social mobility should also facilitate physical mobility.

Mainstream British classrooms have failed to keep pace with pedagogical science. In appearance, they aren't significantly different to what they were a century ago. Perhaps classroom have changed slightly in their configuration but the way in which educators fundamentally use these spaces has not. What's more, the role of architects in designing schools is being steadily dismantled. The most recently example took place in 2014, when the Education Funding Agency introduced baseline designs templates for future school buildings.

Two factors contribute to the way in which children use educational settings: the design of the space itself, and the rules implemented within that space. Often, the ingenuity of the architect is subverted by rash and absurd rules implemented by educators.

I witnessed this firsthand at the school in which I worked in as a supply teacher assistant. The school

Children's drawings of their 'ideal school'

was built in the 1950s and features fifteen, single-storey classrooms which are arranged in three staggered blocks connected by sun-lit corridors and surrounded by multiple playgrounds enveloped by evergreen trees. The building is similar in appearance to much of the municipal architecture of that era, but what makes the school remarkable is that all classrooms are engulfed in natural light and all have near-immediate access to playgrounds.

The architects had created the ideal setting for movement-based learning with a rich connection to the outdoors. However, the way in which the educators used the space during my time there was antithetical to this. Learning primarily took place on the classroom carpet, overseen by the teachers who sat above their level on chairs. The children were treated like objects that needed to be ordered. The carpet design reflected this regimental ordering with a graphic grid, each square differentiated by an insect. The way in which children sat was also dictated: crossed legged and no fidgeting. Failure to comply resulted in further limitation of movement by banishment to the 'thinking island': a euphemism for solitary confinement where the child was forced to sit in silence and watch a sand timer.

The children were not allowed to run, never indoors and rarely even outside. Apart from their allotted thirty minutes of play at lunchtime, running was banned across the campus and access to the playground was limited to five pupils per class. Everything that the educators practised flew in the face of the contemporary science of education and the architecture of the school itself. These absurd practices not only demonstrated the miseducation of educators, but also the overwhelming pressure they were placed under.

The school is located in a neglected corner of London, where around half of all pupils are recipients of free schools meals and over 90% start nursery with language skills below the expected level. Great pressure was placed upon teachers to radically improve children's language skills before the Phonics Screening Test, a compulsory test that took place in all state schools at the end of the children's first year of education. The exam was implemented by the coalition government in 2011 in an attempt to improve national reading standards. Whether or not it has achieved its intended outcome is debatable, but it has certainly resulted in the adoption of the 'teaching to test' method. The playground has, therefore, been turned into just another classroom equipped with tables, writing equipment and books. Perhaps a ban on running will encourage children to write instead!

A school building that seeks to enrich a child's life should structurally invite them to move around the space. No building does that more boldly than Kita Kupferhammer in Frankfurt, which allows children to slide, climb and roll around in the building. Commissioned by the City of Frankfurt in 1989, the children's centre was formerly known as Heddenheim-Nord Kindergarten and was designed by the eccentric artist-architect Friedensreich Hundertwasser. The building's turfed roof gently slopes out of the meadow with two mismatched zinc cupolas perched at the top. Resembling a fantastical stage set, the building is composed of concave brown concrete walls detailed with ceramic mosaic.

Nestled into the northern elevation, upheld by colourful oversized balustrades, is the entrance. The kindergarten occupies the lower floor. Its three main activity rooms each grant access to a gallery. Beneath the cupolas is an after-school study space for older children, which opens on to a rooftop terrace. The playground extends on to the slanted earthen roof by way of built-in steps and a slide – a symbolic gesture of the children's ownership of the space.

The diversity of interior space, with split-level classrooms, and the variety of materials used creates a stimulating environment for the children to explore. The rooms are devoid of right-angles and the windows are arranged haphazardly, creating an unpredictable and enticing learning environment.

It is a stark contrast to standard municipal school buildings; a joyful place that provides a refuge from the harsh realities of the urban environment. It is an exemplar of the refreshing possibility of what schools could be like if the role of the architect in designing them isn't subverted by government officials.

A spatial framework for social mobility must be implemented alongside pedagogic and political reform. With escalating child poverty rates it is imperative that we create nurturing environments that are sensitive to its subjects' developmental wellbeing. Local authorities have already admitted that they have failed since over half of school are in need of improvement. We need regnegade architects and educators to set the conditions of future improvements. It's time to abolish the outdated classroom model and set the children free.

Kita Kupferhammer formerly known as Heddenheim-Nord Kindergarten, by Friedensreich Hundertwasser (1986-1995)

Objet Blah

Tara Okeke

In 1973, Sotheby's auctioned off Robert Scull's bounteous back catalogue of Warhols, Rauschenbergs, Klines and Lichtensteins for an unprecedented profit.

It was watershed moment for the art industry, marking the emergence of a newly 'hyper commercialized' art market. The tenor of this single sale reverberated decades later in the modus operandi of such collectors as Saatchi, Jopling, and Zabludowicz.

45 years later, however, Scull has been supplanted: Banksy is now the most recent force to have reshaped the industry, owing to the recent sale of 'Love Is In The Bin / The Girl With The Balloon' in 2018.

"But it wasn't always this way!" cries the cultural critic – a comment for the ages that has been deployed at cyclical intervals in each epoch. The only result of this comment being the identification of ever-shifting signifiers of progress and regression.

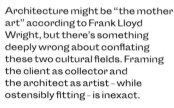

Architecture might be "the mother art" according to Frank Lloyd Wright, but there's something deeply wrong about conflating these two cultural fields. Framing the client as collector and the architect as artist – while ostensibly fitting – is inexact.

The overlaps between art and architecture can be found in their economy. The way in which high-cost, large-scale architecture considers return on investment and adding value bears striking resemblance to the commercial art world. Let's refer to these slick, glossy – but ultimately soulless – creations as objects d'architecture or 'architecture-as-art'.

When we approach architecture as an art object, we follow in the footsteps of such practitioners as Le Corbusier and Bruno Munari.

What's more, architecture-as-art it's underpinned by psychology. Consider the three components of the psyche: the id, ego and superego. Now consider their respective defining traits of (indulgent) instinct, (mediatory) reality and (self-critical) morality. Most architectural products and praxes exhibit one or more of these traits. Apply this to the philosophies of some of the most significant architectural names of our age: Frank 'I'm constantly letting things just evolve' Gehry; Zaha 'a brilliant design will always benefit from the input of others' Hadid; and Neave 'I'm talking politics; maybe I shouldn't be' Brown. Evidently, the prevailing architectural culture in the Western world is one of id and ego.

"But should it always be this way?" Shift the tense. Reframe the thought – from remark to query – and everything changes. We are no longer looking back at what has been – scouting as the cultural critics did for precedents and portents, development and decline – but are instead looking forward to what could be.

What would our world look like if we shifted the focus away from objects d'architecture and more firmly onto architectural interventions that aid and arise from organisation and disruption?

id? **ego?** **superego?**

This is not to say we shouldn't look back before we move on. New Urbanism offers some pertinent lessons on liveability, sustainability and design equity (if one disregards the sleepy Truman Show-like suburban monoculture it can also beget).

Historically, architects have had "the unique privilege and responsibility of housing the one and representing the many" argues Sylvia Lavin in Kissing Architecture. We are all in this together. As such, it behoves us all to keep calling for institutional change, greater transparency, better regulation and for spaces to be "grounded in the experience of true dwelling" once more.

In his 2018 book Palaces For The People, Eric Klinenberg defines social infrastructure as "the physical places and organisations that shape the way people interact", and suggests that it is the missing link in the broad global project of unifying polarized societies, and protecting vulnerable communities and alienated individuals.

These places and organisations – which often take the form of a parks, youth clubs, libraries and so on – tend not to inspire much in the way of aesthetic critique but do wonders to shape an individual's connections with the urban environment and one another.

These are uncertain times, and such a question gives rise to even more uncertainty. Tectonic shifts in the ways in which we communicate, debate and dissent have resulted in vast socio-political fissures and the vilification of those with the courage to organise, mobilise and resist.

Though the road ahead is uncertain, it is still a worthy one to take, for hope "locates itself in the premises of that we don't know what will happen and that in the spaciousness of uncertainty is the room to act," according to writer Rebecca Solnit.

There is a world beyond objet d'architecture. It's dynamic. It's audacious. And it's far from a work of art.

"When you look at hist[ory] every revo[lution] been base[d] redefining means to

"... take a ... ory, almost ... ution has ... around ... what it ... e human."

Indy Johar

Escapades in Consciousness
Reflecting on human beings, architecture and material culture
Samson Séyí Famusan

The machines are not a prophecy, they are here today. In many a hot take, and even in more thorough theses about the mechanisation of jobs, it seems probable that even the creative professions will eventually give way to the creative bots. The real misunderstanding is the idea that AI-designed projects will be better than those designed by humans. No matter the outcome of the idealistically-convoluted, technically-efficient designs, they will still be a product of data, data that was inputted by humans, and this is where errors most commonly occur.

The theory of evolution tells us that everything adapts, however evolution isn't always of a physical nature. All living creatures have adapted their existence for survival but it can be argued that humans have gone past this stage and have instead started to adapt the results of the preceding phenomena via technology, using it to explore physical, psychological and spiritual questions.

However, architecture – one of our most ancient technologies – has never really had a direct link with consciousness. In his book 'The Origin of Consciousness in the Breakdown of the Bicameral Mind', Julian Jaynes asserts that at one time our minds were divided in two and that this influenced the way architecture was executed. His controversial thesis describes the mentality of early humans as bicameral, with one half of the brain issuing commands to the other and thereby giving the impression of a voice speaking – hence stories of gods and spirits conversing with humans. Humans only latterly acquired what we understand as consciousness when the bicameral mind fused in the second millennium BC.

Jaynes argues that what early humans thought was most salient to their being was gods and this was represented in the way their cities and homes were designed. Pre-Bronze Age design revolved around altars or idols, which formed the fulcrum of architecture. In houses the most carefully designed spaces would be where the god's figurine would stand; at times this might even be on higher ground than the rest of the house. In the case of cities, all views and roads led to the temples or palaces.

An issue with Jaynes' attempt to use architecture as evidence for his daring thoughts on the development of consciousness, is that architecture hasn't changed as much over time as his thesis might suggest. The garden city movement, for instance, replicates the assumed structure of the bicameral mind with its distinction of societal functions. The centre of the master plan will always be the commercial and business sectors, with their towers being the main focus; this is surrounded by residential areas on the outskirts. It is not a deep or novel analogy to suggest that materialism and money are new 'gods'; the comparison is long suggested. But what intrigues is that even with a more explored notion of 'self' in the 21st century, architecture is not reflective of recent escapades in our understanding of consciousness.

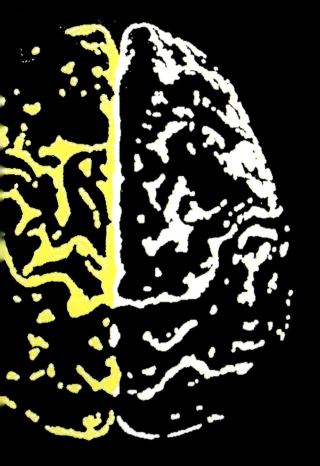

If at first architecture was rooted in community, today its aim lies somewhere on a spectrum between necessity and the intellectually flagrant. Architect Indy Johar has stated that there are certain weaknesses in architecture's systems and strategies that need to be addressed: we need to rediscover what it is to be human, how we are supposed to work, and why we are what we are or going to be. The idea of such questions being part of architectural education may seem fanciful at best but this could be where a plethora of productive lines of thought might originate, and the links between architecture and consciousness could be rebuilt.

Today, the notion of conscious architecture is vaguely gathered under the umbrella of holistic, natural design, but this should be revised. Education in architecture mostly falls into theoretical or practical exercises; at best, it is a merger of both, but this could be taken further. If the curriculum shifted to a balance of the psychological with the material, new disciplinary approaches will begin to arise, and these might also impact on the pressing questions regarding our current relationship with the material world. Our architecture has generally been examined through the lens of how people interact with space but not vice versa. Only rarely have environmentalist critics advised "never bite the hand that feeds you". Our species has become master of materials, bending them to our will, but could there be more to the equation?

It would be an exaggeration to suggest that what we have built today or our knowledge of the built environment is not a feat. Nevertheless, the general sense, inspired by the homogeneity of contemporary architecture, that we have achieved conclusive answers to all our problems, is what has led to the failings of our systems. Why is it that what was designed and built for us to some becomes a bête noire? The jury is out on what we are – evolved multicellular organism rooted in dubiety, spiritual beings having a human experience, or other conclusions that defy comprehension. One clear step is that for all the available technology and the pace at which we continue to build, the core of our knowledge still requires examination. Architecture should be defined as philosophy seeking an answer through design.●

Figures of Thought
Thomas Aquilina

A letter to his mentor, **Adrian Lahoud**, the dean of the architecture school at the RCA, following their conversations on mental health and architecture.

The key question: What are the key sites of social struggle from the perspective of the architect today?

22nd February 2019
London

Dear Adrian,

I've been thinking about the question you asked at our event last summer: what are the key sites of social struggle from the perspective of the architect today? I didn't realise it then, but I think this question has been at the centre of conversations you and I have maintained in recent months — and the difficulty I've had in coming to terms with my mental impasse.

In this letter, I'd like to reflect broadly on your question by outlining some preliminary ideas, starting with my private headspace. Like an obstacle course, I'll try to navigate what it's like to be caught up and disturbed by mental health as an architectural designer. And how it's also made me interested in the role of urban guardianship for architects. I suppose we can consider these ideas as 'figures of thought.'

<u>The Personal is (Always) Social</u>
As we've discussed, in the last few years, I've struggled with a seemingly unending cycle of mental health issues and the anxiety around this. I've become aware of the fragility of mental health, as well as the

physical symptoms: eczematic skin, alopecia, pins-and-needles, non-stop scratching, lethargy. In each instance, the internal is expressed visibly.

For me, mental health is the key arena of social struggle. It might be something I experience as a deeply private anguish but it is profoundly public. My headspace manifested within a layered set of class and race, and social relationships. In other words, the terrain of struggle is always contingent upon its context.

The Architect as a General Practitioner

I believe the context and culture of architectural education and practice can often exacerbate mental health struggles. When production is regularly shaped by competition and exploitation and judgement, an indifference to care and nurture can fester. This interests me in what role the architect might take in a restorative future orientation. To use a thought experiment, can an architect be more akin to a medical general practitioner?

In this architect-as-GP model, architects would understand their local urban environments and have a duty to design as well as care for it. Perhaps they'd work for a community land trust and be allocated 1,000 dwellings for a 10-year term? The built environment would be cultivated whilst social relationships nurtured — and the architect's generalist role would be strengthened.

I suppose this would require a radical questioning of the political economy of architecture, and that suggests psychological distress is also deeply political.

Fragility is not Failure

As a black Caribbean male, with mental illness in my family, the statistical odds are stacked against me. Despite this, when I first recognised the fragility of my mental health, I thought of it as some irrational state of mind — a sort of omnipresent yet obscure sense of failure. But it's quite a powerful place to be and has become an opportunity for self-awareness.

Even if, in reality, fragility is only allowed in certain contexts where people can trust each other (like writing this to you). As a mentor, your conversations with me have opened up an inwardness and a chance to think in a different space.

Thank you — Thomas

P.S. For the playlist, I recommend Kondi Band (Afro-electronic...)

Fail better.